HOUSEBREAKING MEISHAN PIGS IS POSSIBLE

Cultivating Clean Habits: Housebreaking Success with Meishan Pigs

SARAH VINCENT

Table of Contents

CHAPTER ONE 3
  PREFACE 3
  Origins and History 3
CHAPTER TWO 7
  ANATOMY AND EXTERNAL LOOK 7
    COLORS 8
    HEAD 8
    EARS 9
    SNOUT (THE NOSE) 9
    WEIGHT 9
    HEIGHT 10
    TEETH 10
    TUSKS 11
    NAILS AND HOOVES 13
    TAIL 13
CHAPTER THREE 15
  Qualities and Individuality 15
    Sentient beings 19
  Meishan Pigs Are Very Vigilant 23
CHAPTER FOUR 27
  Housebreaking Meishan pigs is possible 27

Empathetic	28
They are able to detect sadness	29
They might be delicate	30
Life Expectancy and Breeding	32
Children	34
Life expectancy	34
Environment and Habitat	35
Natural Setting	36
Surroundings	36
Dietary Needs	38
Positives and Negatives	42
ADVANTAGES	42
DIFFERENCES	47
THE END	52

CHAPTER ONE
PREFACE

Large drooping ears are another characteristic of Meishan pigs that many owners adore and seek for. Many find them much cuter because of their droopy ears.

What therefore can be learned about Meishan pigs? You can discover all the information you require concerning these wrinkled, droopy-eared pigs in this post.

Origins and History

As previously mentioned, Meishan pigs are native to China and are now uncommon outside of that nation. Currently, the breed is regarded as "critically endangered."

The lack of use for the aforementioned breed is most likely the reason for their population reduction. Compared to other breeds of pigs, Meishan pigs develop more slowly and have more fat on them.

One of the earliest heritage breeds of domesticated pigs is the Meishan pig. It's probable that most farmers preferred the other well-known and comparable breeds, such as Berkshire pigs, when it came to producing livestock.

The breed, which belongs to the Taihu Chinese breed of pigs, is named after the Chinese prefecture of Meishan.

In the US, meishan pigs are mostly utilized for breeding operations and scientific studies. The possibility of extinction may have led to the termination of the investigation.

The Meishan line of pigs is currently being preserved by conservation organizations in an effort to return the population from endangered to normal.

CHAPTER TWO

ANATOMY AND EXTERNAL LOOK

It's time to go into further detail about these cuddly, wrinkly pigs' bodies now that we have a better understanding of their past.

The Meishan breed of pigs is often small to medium sized, although the original Taihu breed of pigs is typically huge. They also grow slowly and acquire fat more readily.

In spite of this, they have a highly robust body that makes them resistant to some illnesses and enables them to eat roughage, something that not all pig breeds are capable of.

COLORS

Only dark hues are associated with Meishan breeds. Just two hues are typical: absolute black and dark brown. Meishan pigs that are crossbred or mixed may have a different hue.

HEAD

Because of the wrinkles, their faces appear larger than they actually are.

EARS

In addition to being frequently huge, ears can also get fairly long and always droop downward.

SNOUT (THE NOSE)

They have upturned noses with light-colored, possibly peach or pink, markings.

WEIGHT

A mature Meishan pig weighs an average of 61 kg (134 pounds) on its body.

HEIGHT

An adult Meishan pig's maximum height is 22 inches (57.8 cm), and its maximum chest measurement is 39 inches (100 cm).

TEETH

Meishan pigs can bite quite hard at food despite having regular, non-sharp teeth. After birth, all pigs often have their needle-sharp teeth trimmed within hours or minutes.

After then, normal teeth take the place of the sharp teeth.

TUSKS

All pigs, including domestic varieties like Meishan pigs, develop tusks. No exceptions—male or female, wild or domestic.

The tusks of females are typically smaller and shorter, and they hardly ever get long or large enough to protrude from their mouths. This characteristic made it one of the simple methods for determining the gender of pigs in the wild.

The tusks function as a pig's attacking and defense weapon.

However, since they are useless in confinement, domestic pigs typically have their tusks removed entirely.

In case you didn't know, the tusk is regarded as a component of the teeth and is a portion of the jawbones. This implies that their tusks will not regrow if you chop them off.

Trimming, on the other hand, is a distinct task performed solely for pig care.

NAILS AND HOOVES

Meishan pigs may require clipping of their "dewclaws" and hooves. A pig has to have its fur trimmed at least once a year on average.

Pigs kept indoors will need more trimming, whereas outside pigs with a firm foundation may just need fewer trimming sessions.

TAIL

Meishan pigs are known for having long, straight tails that they can curl. Although there are many hypotheses explaining why pigs curl their tails, there is no real answer.

A pig's tail is only known to be used to ward off insects like flies. Its purpose is to go to places where their tongue and legs cannot.

CHAPTER THREE

Qualities and Individuality

Meishan pigs' outward appearance could give the impression that they are depressing. Their huge, drooping ears conceal their eyes, and they frequently have their head lowered due to their dark coloring.

In contrast to other breeds, they are recognized for being incredibly gentle and silent pigs. They are frequently complimented for having a laid-back disposition that facilitates easier handling at work.

While other breeds of pigs frequently oink or grunt, Meishan pigs hardly ever make noise, and they are often praised for it.

Once you get beyond their unusual appearance, you will be enthralled with how tranquil and sweet they can be—even though they might not be as appealing as the other well-known breeds.

In addition, the faces of their piglets or infants mimic the wrinkled faces of popular pug dogs.

The "trend" of enjoying animals with wrinkled bodies and faces is growing in popularity, but we want to show that caring for these creatures should be about giving them your whole heart, not just following a fad.

Compared to other submissive breeds of pigs, they have a completely different personality. Meishan pigs are sometimes referred to as "sleepyheads" since they would much sooner nap than interact with other pigs.

Unless they are still piglets, these gentle giants have never been observed attacking or fighting with other pigs, animals, or even humans. Given their young age, piglets are capable of playing fight and creating some noise.

People will be shocked to learn how different Meishan pigs are from regular pigs once they reach adulthood.

The majority of pigs are regarded as among nature's "escape artists," yet Meishan pigs have never gotten in the way of walls, fences, or other obstructions that would keep them from moving on.

As long as they are secure, they will remain where they can.

Sentient beings

They are not only incredibly gentle creatures, but also highly intelligent. They are quick learners and have a large memory, just like any other pig.

It is a known fact that pigs were ranked sixth in the world's intelligence rankings.

Their small to medium-sized frame conceals a large brain and a compassionate nature! Who knew that they have a startling degree of knowledge hidden beneath their adorable, wrinkled face and body?

One of the smartest species we've ever seen, chimpanzees, can be outwitted by pigs as well! Meishan pigs, on the other hand, prefer to let other animals win because they are not competitive swine. They are capable of being that tranquil.

Aside from their excellent memory, Meishan pigs can also amaze you with how quickly they take things up and can learn new things.

In addition to coming in fifth place globally, surveys and study in the scientific community have shown that the typical pig's IQ is equivalent to that of a two-year-old human child.

They found that, in contrast to dogs and chimps, pigs can focus better and achieve greater success rates when it comes to tests and difficulties.

Certain dogs are considered to be difficult or even arrogant, therefore not all dogs are as quick learners as pigs. When it comes to training, many dogs can be stubborn even though they are often docile.

In contrast, pigs appear to learn things on their own without needing to be forced. Because they can concentrate better, they typically pick things up more quickly. Dogs' lively disposition makes them readily sidetracked.

Meishan Pigs Are Very Vigilant

Being prey animals is another reason why pigs, including Meishan pigs, are extremely intelligent in comparison to other animals.

Meishan pigs were tamed from the moment they were born, so they have never known the wild, but they have kept their wild and organic characteristics.

We are now shocked by the abilities of pigs, a prey, as we have been accustomed to keeping and raising predatory animals like dogs and cats for the most part! It's time we gave these creatures a chance to feel appreciated and understood.

Because they must be more vigilant than predators, prey creatures may evolve more delicate lifestyles. They must possess more intelligence than their nimble and powerful predators.

Pigs may have developed higher intelligence by adjusting to their environment and figuring out how to trick their predators.

Predators typically don't need to be vigilant because they feel at ease in most places and don't have to work as hard to find food as prey does.

It's because you get desperate to hang on for survival when you're constantly on edge. Top performers, on the other hand, often take things for granted and lose sight of the purpose of obstacles.

Life's challenges help you grow stronger. If they have a strong mind, they will have a higher chance of surviving even if they are prey animals.

CHAPTER FOUR

Housebreaking Meishan pigs is possible

Meishan pigs can be housebroken if necessary, despite the fact that they are mostly raised for breeding and kept as livestock on farms.

Pigs learn faster than dogs, according to a lot of pig owners. Pigs in general, including Meishan pigs, can be housebroken. They might pick up various new skills, such playing catch and using the litter box.

Additionally, it has been demonstrated that training pigs using the "treat rewarding" strategy is highly effective.

Empathetic

Meishan pigs, for example, are intelligent enough to have compassion in proportion to their intelligence. Their cognitive abilities enable them to experience both good and negative emotions.

They can therefore experience pain, depression, excitement, and a host of other emotions! For this reason, a great deal of individuals are persuaded that the inhumane treatment of livestock pigs ought to halt.

They are not mindless beings that are meant to be utilized as tools or things for our personal benefit. Meishan pigs, like pigs of other breeds, should receive equitable treatment.

They are able to detect sadness
Pigs have the ability to sense sadness in other animals, in their friends, or in their human masters. When they do, they often comfort them by consoling them.

Meishan pigs can sense when a friend dies, when they are abandoned, or when they are left behind. When they are grieving a loss or are just missing something or someone, they might get so sad, dejected, and lonely that they cry real tears.

They might be delicate

You should anticipate that they would act like children since they are nearly as intelligent as children. Meishan pigs are prone to boredom when left alone or discomfort when housed in an awkward space, among other things.

They have the capacity to become domineering, spoiled, obstinate, or manipulative. They never use violence, though. Meishan pigs don't attack people unless they feel really scared or provoked in a corner.

A pig who experiences mistreatment or cruelty WILL remember it. They are able to retain resentment and recall the faces of their tormentors, but they are also capable of gratitude and remembering people who were there for them.

Because Meishan pigs may be emotionally sensitive as well, their conduct requires their owners to be emotionally ready, which is part of what makes them such attractive animals.

Pigs need to be loved and cared for with sincerity!

Life Expectancy and Breeding

The population of Meishan pigs fell when most farmers concluded there was little use for the breed that would benefit them.

Nevertheless, each breed has advantages and disadvantages of its own, which are discussed at the conclusion of this post.

Meishan pigs often reach sexual maturity at 2 to 3 months of age, which is 3 months earlier than the typical 6 months compared to most other breeds of pigs, despite their slow growth and excess of fat.

They can support up to 22 newborn pigs at a time, which makes them useful for reproduction. They also have at least 18 to 22 teats where their liter (offspring) can suckle.

One of their special talents that sets them apart from other pigs is this.

Children

Meishan pigs are well-known for having a large capacity. They have a high pregnancy success rate and can give birth to 15 to 22 litters (piglets). They are also excellent mothers.

Life expectancy

The typical lifespan of a Meishan pig is fifteen to twenty years.

Fewer individuals wish to keep Meishan pigs because of their population's constant decline. Conservation organizations assert, however, that with the right care, Meishan can reach their prime.

Based on the available data, we may conclude that pigs can sometimes outlive their predicted lifespan if they are well-cared for and shown affection.

Environment and Habitat

Meishan pigs thrive best in regions with moderate temperatures. As long as the weather doesn't hurt them, they may grow practically anyplace and are neither finicky nor difficult to manage.

Natural Setting

Natural habitat for Meishan pigs is comparable to that of other common pigs.

The majority of pigs' natural habitats are often damp woods, marshes, and woodlands, particularly oak forests and areas with an abundance of seeds.

Surroundings

All pigs, but small to medium breeds such as Meishan pigs, will want to live in climate-friendly areas. They can still be vulnerable to extreme cold or heat, even if they work best in mild or chilly settings.

Since these pigs are prey, any potential predators must be kept at bay. Fences are necessary to keep out animals like wolves, coyotes, and even common stray dogs if they have a large area outside for grazing.

Since most pigs are sensitive to inclement weather, they need to be kept out of high heat and bitter cold. They need to be protected from all types of storms and rain.

Dietary Needs

Like other pig breeds, Meshian pigs have comparable dietary requirements. The general diet of Meshian pigs is as follows:

1. Commercial Pig Feed: Meshian pigs may be fed a commercial pig feed that has been particularly prepared to meet their nutritional needs. The diet should be balanced. These feeds come in pellet or meal form and are commonly supplied with a

combination of grains, protein sources, vitamins, and minerals. You should speak with an animal nutritionist or veterinarian to find out what kind and quantity of commercial pig feed is best for your Meshian pig.

2. Fruits and Vegetables: A range of fruits and vegetables are also available for Meshian pigs to eat. Apples, carrots, cucumbers, sweet potatoes, pumpkins, and leafy greens (like spinach or lettuce) are typical choices. These ought to be served in moderation and divided

into portions that are manageable for consumption.

3. Hay and Forage: Meshian pigs' digestive systems require access to high-quality hay, such as timothy or alfalfa hay. Hay is high in dietary fiber and supports healthy gut flora. Permitting them to graze on grass and other plants in pastures or foraging areas can also be advantageous.

4. Water: Meshian pigs should always have access to clean, fresh water. For hydration and to

facilitate digestion, they require continuous access to water.

It's crucial to remember that the precise nutritional needs and feeding guidelines for Meshian pigs might change based on a number of variables, including age, weight, activity level, and general health. To create a suitable feeding schedule catered to your Meshian pig's specific requirements, it is always essential to seek the advice of a licensed animal nutritionist or veterinarian.

Positives and Negatives

All animals, including humans, are flawed in some way. Every pet has advantages and disadvantages. Meishan pigs may offer more advantages than disadvantages in and of themselves, as we will elucidate.

ADVANTAGES

1. Little upkeep

Indeed, caring for these Meishan pigs is quite simple.

They don't require a lot of room, are immune to several diseases, are not picky eaters, and have natural foraging abilities that enable them to locate food on their own outside, so they are not high maintenance.

But just because kids are able to eat anything, even junk food, doesn't mean we should give them anything. Even yet, some foods may be detrimental to their health and compromise their immune system.

More to the point, installing fences to keep these pigs under your supervision costs less because they don't usually escape farms or their living quarters!

They are able to survive on their own and spend the majority of the day sleeping as long as they are given access to sufficient food, water, and a stable shelter in addition to protection from potential predators.

2. Good maternal abilities

Meishan pigs are capable of bearing up to 22 piglets at a time, which is advantageous for farmers because the mother pigs can raise and tend to the young without inadvertently hurting them.

With a Meishan pig, accidents like inadvertently sitting on the piglet or choking them are quite rare. They are also adept at feeding their young.

A pig with strong maternal instincts is typically a competent caregiver for other abandoned animals, such as kittens and pups. Pigs owned by numerous rescuers are available to act as volunteer foster mothers.

3. Kind, tranquil creatures

A Meishan pig will sooner hide and flee than defend itself when it is confronted. A Meishan pig has never been known to assault a human.

Despite my best efforts, I was unable to find any instances of attacks on other pigs or animals; these pigs are always reported as kind and calm. They have never hurt or attacked someone else.

They can be wonderful friends because they will never hurt you, so we should never hurt them in return.

DIFFERENCES

1. Gradual expansion

In order to earn money more quickly, some farmers would rather produce faster-growing varieties. This makes total sense, which is why most people find Meishan pigs' sluggish growth to be undesirable.

Despite their slower growth rate, they are ready for reproduction at a much younger age—2 to 3 months—than most breeds.

Meishan pigs still have good birth success rates and produce a large number of liters (piglets) despite their early reproductive stage.

2. Lots much fat

Their abundance of fat is another reason why some farmers do not like them. Even though they are not picky eaters, they need to be fed properly because they quickly gain weight and become unusable.

3. Not as gregarious as other animals

Sometimes, energetic and vivacious animals are preferred by their owners. This implies that people might think uninteresting creatures like Meishan pigs, who are incredibly calm, tranquil, and submissive.

This is entirely situational, though, and doesn't truly represent a drawback for Meishan pigs.

Is raising endangered pigs permissible?

The legality of owning a pig depends largely on the state of its population, but generally speaking, owning any kind of pig involves obtaining a license, which entails becoming registered and authorized.

Pigs must be registered and licensed in the majority of US and UK regions, whether they are being kept as pets or as livestock.

Certain licenses or additional criteria may be necessary for rare, unusual, or endangered breeds.

It is important to visit or phone your local animal welfare authorities to find out the most recent information about raising pigs in your area. Every state or region may have different laws and rules.

THE END

Printed in the USA
CPSIA information can be obtained
at www.ICGtesting.com
LVHW012329120524
780098LV00005B/154